Black Men:

How They Date, Love and Marry - or Not

Chris Nazareth

Cedar Avenue Press ~ Atlanta, Ga

Black Men

Published by Cedar Avenue Press

Copyright © 2011 by Chris Nazareth

All rights reserved. No part of this book may be reproduced or transmitted in any form or by any means, electronic or mechanical, including photocopying, recording, or by any information storage or retrieval system, without permission in writing from the publisher.

Published by Cedar Avenue Press, Atlanta, Ga
Member of Southern Bay Publishing Group, a division of Nazareth Neely, LLC

www.CedarAvenuePress.com

I dedicate this book to my daughter Zahra in the hope that it will not be needed when she becomes a woman.

Acknowledgments

I would like to thank Bella, DeKimberlen, Kaye, Naima, Angie, Neca, and Nikki My guides into and through the process.

Foreword

In this age of social media, it has been made clear that finding and maintaining a quality relationship is the most common challenge amongst men and women in their 30's. A crisis has surfaced and been made public, but all is not lost.

This book is a brilliant snapshot of the past and how the will to survive and prosper in the United States as a unified group, coming out of slavery and civil rights, has systematically been disassembled before we ever got the blueprint. In fact, there aren't even any instructions, at least none we will ever receive in the box of our lives.

The only recourse is to understand where we are now, how we got here, and how to unlearn all of the habits and dysfunctions that have been glorified in this current society through pop culture and media. Chris offers a chance to start that process with this book, not only in how we treat and view ourselves, but in our treatment of others.

Through the love and growth of self, the compassion and understanding of others, and the capacity to change our behavior patterns, we can indeed increase the chances of finding a suitable mate and life partner.

-Shaun Amin

Table of Contents

Introduction 1

Why Cheating Is Absolutely Normal 9

Dating These Days Can Ruin Your Life! 17

Understanding the Black Man 22

Understanding the Black Woman 59

Racial Differences in Human Sexuality 79

7 Steps To Change a Black Man's Life 91

7 Steps To Change a Black Woman's Love Life 101

The Best Kind of Man 132

Getting Your Man! 137

Bibliography 149

Introduction

Where we are as a people is fragmented because of our inability to date with any success. This may sound crazy, but if you look at things the way I see them, you will quickly understand my point. Dating and the act of repeated exposure to the opposite sex carry with it many functions: companionship, sex, entertainment, and tradition. All these motivations are important, but the ultimate goal is to get to know if this person is someone with whom you would like to spend most of your time. In other words, if this person is someone you would call your man or your woman.

Becoming a couple is the natural prerequisite to marriage which, in turn, leads to children, grandchildren, aunts, uncles, and cousins. In short, dating is what creates families, and we all know that healthy family structures are what we lack as a community. So then, this problem must be traced back to its roots – dating. Dating has been a sore subject in the African American community for the last two generations, and it is getting worse. Why is it that Black men have such a bad reputation when it comes to dating?

This book is about Black men, dating and their role in the most significant crisis in Black America – the diminishing Black family. It offers insight into areas of their psyche, emotions, and behavior, previously unknown to most, with the intention of bringing understanding to the ways in which they love, date, and marry – or not.

Unlike Daniel Patrick Moynihan's study The Negro Family in the U.S.: The Case for National Action, this book seeks not to lay the blame for the crisis of the Black family at the feet of African American women. It does, however, share a theme that chattel slavery and the resulting economic imbalance influenced the family far more than did the American experience alone. It also draws conclusions that point to the Black man as a missing variable, but explains why, rather than blames.

While there are many in the social sciences who have attempted to understand, explain, and offer solutions to the crisis of the diminishing Black family in the past, their work is often of an academic nature and covers particular elements of dysfunction within the Black community. Since their work requires references to academic concepts, it goes unread by those who need both understanding and solutions most desperately. W.E.B. DuBois, E. Franklin Frazier, Robert Hill, Paula Giddings, and many others contributed scholarly work to the body of knowledge that informs this book to a great degree, but missed the audience that would benefit most from the tremendously important information they amassed.

Very recently, however, writers and scholars such as Julia and Nathan Hare, Audrey Chapman, and Patricia Dixon have approached this devastating issue from what I consider the root of the problem - the male/female relationship. Their varied perspectives cover the contemporary angst that we find among African American women, the overbearing weight of racism, and the historical and spiritual dynamics of relationships that have "real world" application for the reader. This book has a bent toward the latter but with an "every woman" delivery. It is rooted in the excellent work of these scholars and others.

There are also pop books that have been written which seek to add the authors' two cents, usually from either popular notions or their own opinions. Writers such as Shahrazad Ali have produced popular books that offered some important kernels of truth, but may have come across as distasteful to many because of her brutal honesty and what some perceived as generalizations.

Introduction

More recently, Steve Harvey's books have continued to be tremendously successful, and are full of the "down-home" wisdom of a person who pays full attention to the current events and the lessons that life has offered. In my opinion, his books contain a lot of what Black women already "know" and as such, Harvey is preaching to the choir. I also find his solutions tend to reinforce the dual-role lifestyle and the misunderstanding of Black men's shortcomings that are at the heart of many issues.

Hill Harper offers his take on the state of relations in an honest yet gentle way. He addresses the communication barrier that exists between Black men and women. Hill also offers valid solutions for the seeming insecurity between the sexes and give options to those who may feel like giving up.

With this book, I will try to create a version of what the social scientists offer if it were written in the spoken voice. It is not formatted for

Black Men:

research or teaching at the university level; what it contains is the synthesis of the existing literature, data, anecdotal evidence, and my informed opinion. It is a conversation between you and me.

Introduction

Why Cheating Is Absolutely Normal

"All men cheat. Why don't women accept this and enjoy the rest of life with their men?" Anonymous

There is an instinctual drive in humans behind almost all of their behaviors. The response to these basic instincts are seen as everyday behavior but with the human intellect as an instrument of control. Using morality, tradition, and social norms, humans control their behavior by engaging and encouraging those social drives which correspond with their cultures and suppressing or hiding those drives which are contrary.

The drive for sex is one of the strongest of the human instincts, often over-riding even the instinct for survival. Sex, however, is really no different from any other human drive – like food and water. It is profoundly significant in the development of the human being both socially and genetically.

When sex is engaged in properly, with intellectual, moral and ethical values of the culture, there is no cheating involved. This, of course, is based on the social constructs of that culture and not on the natural design of human beings. Human beings have only one consideration when sex is involved when you remove all of the various mechanisms of social control – survival of the species. To acquire the best genes for the next generation, the gene pool must be mixed as much as possible.

There are hardly any cultural roles that do not involve sex. A doctor with your health concerns or a lawyer with marriage/divorce/crime issues can have sex as the subject. A priest or minister with moral concerns or parents discussing sex issues with children has sex potentially imbedded within. It follows that cultural differences also influence the differences in sexual behavior. This is because they may have differing ways of understanding law, health, religion, and sex. These differences can be found in the structure of family life, and with the very different patterns of cultural origin, many distinct sexual behavior patterns arose.

Although modern (Western) ideology assumes and promotes the individual as the unit of human culture, it is really the male-female bonded pair and their children who represent this idea. Also contrary to Western ideology is the fact that there has been, throughout human history, more than one bonded pair per male.

I can imagine that this seems unreasonable and primitive, but it has been, and continues to be the norm for much of the human race. Think of when you hear of cheating in a relationship – do you automatically think it's the woman doing the cheating? You might say "well women cheat too," and of course this is the case, but it is the man who cheats as a matter of his normal course. A woman needs a reason to cheat most of the time, and a man only needs an opportunity. This is perfectly normal and is actually the way we are designed.

The biological reason men cheat is to make the gene pool as varied and complex as possible. This is nature's way of ensuring the survival of the species by adding as many unrelated possible mates for future generations.

A couple that is not distantly related is less likely to have the same carrier genes for inherited disorders. In the case of both parents having carrier genes for the same trait, their children may express the disorder that would have remained dormant if only one parent was a carrier.

Disorders like cystic fibrosis or sickle cell anemia, for example, are avoided by diluting the gene pool as much as possible. This is only accomplished when men impregnate as many different women as possible - this idea is called *genetic diversity.*

On the other hand, women may cheat a bit less, and when they do, it is because of some perceived lack from her current partner. This lack goes to the heart of the matter of female cheating, and it also speaks to the way in which women connect emotionally through sexual relationships while men do not.

The sense of lack that drives women to cheat is related to their built-in desire to be taken care of. For a woman, the act of sex brings with it the possibility of pregnancy. For most of human history we have had to contend with the struggle to eat, stay dry and warm, and to keep safe from predators and other humans. Under such challenging conditions, being pregnant or with a young child can be very dangerous. Without someone to care for her safety, food and shelter, death was a risk that was not uncommon.

Clearly, sex for a woman became an investment, not just the frivolous and pleasurable act that it was for a man. After a sexual encounter

Black Men:

woman may need help in the form of food, shelter and protection for years, whereas a man needs only a cold drink and eight hours sleep.

So, when a woman feels a sense of lack, her subconscious instinct is to begin to seek other opportunities that give her a sense of more consistent support. A man just wants to spread his "seed" all over the place. But understand, men are made this way and the instructions are written right into their DNA. They think they just want sex, but the subconscious is driving them to make as many babies with as many different sets of DNA as possible.

Dating These Days Can Ruin Your Life!

It seems that we go through a cycle of dating which involves either random or staged meetings, putting on the mask and character of what one's self-image considers attractive, going through semi-scripted dialogue and, finally, getting involved sexually.

This game is played over and over, sometimes ending in one-night stands, lifelong marriages, and most often – serial monogamy. This serial monogamy, the act of dating one person exclusively but changing the one person you are dating every six months to a year, is the most detrimental of the types of relationships we tend to have.

Black Men:

It gets family and friends involved, it gets emotions involved and it often creates financial ties that become a problem after the relationship has ended.

Because of the hopeful outlook people have when relationships start, children are often conceived during episodes of serial monogamy. This has severe implications on both single motherhood and the reproductive health of our women.

Often the man in this short-term love affair calls it quits upon hearing the news of a pregnancy. This urges many women to abort the child in light of a future not shared with a responsible father. This oft-repeated aborting wreaks havoc on our women's reproductive organs and has both short-term (fibroids and cysts) and long-term (sterility and cancer) implications on their overall health and lifestyle. This does not take into account the mental and emotional anguish that

Black women suffer from repeatedly having their hearts broken.

Some would say that back in the day things were different. In the past, African Americans had a sort of code of ethics that we observed, at least publicly, concerning our dating behavior. There was a process called courting. In the tradition of courting, a man, usually in his early twenties, attempted to win the affection of a young woman by following a series of pre-defined rituals. There were many variations of a common theme which consisted of finding out if she is even remotely interested, identifying any other suitors, and most importantly – getting the approval of her father.

These days, the ritual lives more commonly in reruns of the Cosby Show than in reality. In fact, I have serious doubt that it will ever become the norm and believe it will probably become passé and "old fashioned" in the near future. There are no rituals to speak of that we observe these days. The parents are informed as a matter of course and, if they disapprove, it will likely have no effect other than keeping the couple at arm's length from the parents, thus causing family pressures that strain the relationship.

Dating These Days Can Ruin Your Life

Understanding the Black Man

In an effort to survive the brutal methods of control that slave owners used such as lynching, shooting, castration, tarring, arson, rape, and battery, African American women sought to protect their boys by sheltering them and teaching them to keep a low profile. This has produced and continues to produce what we now collectively think of as "sorry-ass men."

When African people were shipped to North and South America, the people who controlled and sold them used techniques to "break" them, as you would break a horse that was recently captured from the wild. When breaking a horse, a breaker would ride the horse and destroy the horse's will to defend its life. This was accomplished by giving the horse an outcome that did not fit with its natural expectations. Naturally, a horse expects anything with any sense will run from a thousand-pound whirlwind of sharp hooves and teeth.

In breaking a horse, the cowhand would remain on its back it released all its fury. The horse would immediately accept the new reality. One in which men ride their backs, tell them where they go, when they go, and what they do. Thus begins the horse's life as property.

In the case of a human, this breaking takes place in a much more brutal fashion. A "breaker" finds the strongest male of the newly kidnapped Africans, and pulls him in front of an audience of other captives. Chains are placed on each of the man's legs and then attached to horses facing in opposite directions. He is covered in tar, then feathered, and set afire. The horses panic to get away from the flames and the man is literally torn in two. This is the most brutal form of being tarred and feathered.

Another method used by slave trainers is the lash. Also known as the bullwhip, this weapon was used to bring excited bulls into submission. Think about it. A bull covered in a leather hide can be hurt by a whip. Imagine what this bullwhip can do to human skin. This is not your daddy's belt!

In a typical whipping, the audience is gathered and a strong man is pulled out as the example. He is beaten to within an inch of his life. As he cries and screams, the women and children watch; as this strong man loses bowel and urine control, the women and children watch; as he begs the white slave driver for the life that only God is supposed to give and take away, the women and children watch.

Seeing such "breaking" techniques in action has profound effects on the psyche of all watching. Not only does it instill a lifelong terror in the children, but it also weakens the resolve of any man with ideas of future actions against his captors. Most importantly, it etches a permanent memory on the minds of ALL the black women in attendance. The memory of a black woman is very keen when she decides to alter her behavior with a particular person. Black women may forgive, but they NEVER forget, and they never deal with that person in quite the same way again.

That experience replays itself throughout a black woman's life. A strong man is brought forth, perhaps as a display of strength. An audience is gathered in typical fashion for a show, and then something goes terribly wrong. The strong man is now not only captured, but is shown to be a weakling that cannot defend his own life much less be the protector of his wife and child. Therefore, the black woman's expectations, just as the horse's, have been redefined.

She can no longer see the power associated with a man being a leader, a warrior, a planner, or a great speaker, because she has seen what has happened to these types of men. Even if at a subconscious level, her expectations are permanently altered to fit the new reality where the white men in her life are strong and powerful, and the Black men are weak and helpless. This control of Black men by their oppressors' violent actions is known as institutional decimation – the use of murder and violence to eliminate the threat of Black men.

Simultaneously, she notices that weak, quiet, or shy men are never pulled from the crowd in the way that the strong men are. The pride associated with being a strong man is what gives them away in a crowd. They stand a little taller, frown a little harder, and move a little slower when told to do so. Breaking happened at the end of every voyage from Africa, bringing about generation after generation of Black men, women and children suffering through this sick cycle of altering and, to some degree, reversing what is normal human behavior.

This concept is sometimes reinforced during the life as a slave on a plantation. Imagine, for a moment, a middle-aged white man with a middle-aged white wife on a hot summer night in the not-so-deep South. They live in a home with young teenage Black girls and curvaceous adult Black women living in the backyard – Black girls and women who they own. If the white man has any lust for them, he can project it any and every time he wants because he is uninhibited by morals. After all, they are less than human; they are merely property.

Imagine for a moment you live on one of the plantations. Imagine you live every day of your life at the whim of some man who bears you no good will. Think for a moment of your mother being raped one night, your 14-year-old sister being raped the following night, and as the sun falls tonight, you know you're next. There is no 911 you can call, no sheriff, no social services...nothing! There is no one to help you keep from getting beaten and forced into disgusting and shameful acts by your owner's friends and relatives. There is no one to keep your little sister from getting pregnant again - no one except the Black man in your life.

Rape, which was so common during slavery, was not only the catalyst for the 29 shades of black in this country, but it also led to many hangings, tortures, castrations, etc. Sometimes, there is a limit to what a man can take. Life and limb may become minor issues in light of the circumstances. Witnessing your wife, daughter, or sister being a victim of serial gang rape may be one of those circumstances.

What the enslaved men learned from the breaking experience forced them to suppress thoughts of defending the women in their lives. They would turn a blind eye, walk away, or mentally block out the reality of such occurrences. Even within our families today, we have extremely light-skinned great-aunts and uncles, grandmothers, or grandfathers that bear resemblance to no one in the family because they, or one of their immediate parents, was a product of owner/"boss" sexual relations. This is the norm because of the lack of deterrent force in the Black men. We cover the shame of it by saying, "my Grandmother was half Cherokee," which is true only about half the time.

While most men did nothing obvious to protect their women, some men were unable to contain their feelings about the sexual predation happening around them. They knew what the outcome would be, so they often went "all out" to appease their rage. These men knew that any violent action against their captors would result in death, often by public torture. The women knew not all men could remain docile, and that some men were born with a character devoid of fear. They knew, sometimes, that the fathers of some children were less likely to produce punks! They also knew, all too well, that under the conditions in which they lived, it was easy for some brothers to "snap." The women had to protect their children from this type of behavior. They had to make sure that their boys would never have their penises cut off and stuffed in their mouths or endure any of the other ritualized murders that were committed as retribution for any attempt to defend the Black woman. They ensured that these boys would never have a strong sense of empathy – they would never love TOO much.

The trouble began then. At some point, hundreds of years ago, Blacks adopted a standardized but unwritten method of murder-proofing boys. Just as a standard method of cooking soul food and having church service in every corner of Black America is uniform without committee, so were the survival strategies employed to save the lives of our men.

The mothers of young Black boys began to instill a sense in the boys that they need not protect their mothers, and that they also should not desire to excel at anything that would draw unwanted attention. Mothers, instead, taught their boys to be not so loud, not so proud, not so strong and not so angry. If a boy had to be angry, he had to be angry with anyone except the "white men up yonder!" The boy had to bottle it up and hold it in until he was around only other Blacks.

Mothers drummed it into the heads of young boys so well and for so long, that even today; the roughest, toughest gang banger on the streets will kill 30 black men before he will turn his gun on a white man! In protecting them, these great-, great- and a few more great-grandmothers of ours have trained our men into perpetual boyhood.

It follows that the women often "put down" the boys in a public display of their uselessness and lack of worth. This, too, was a way of protecting their sons from harm by keeping them from being sold away, as no one would put a premium on a stupid, lazy, or roguish slave.

One might say, "That was 300 years ago!" or "That slavery stuff is long gone!" and sound logically justified; however, I have an analogy that makes my point crystal clear. A mother, Tonya, was teaching her daughter, Ashley, how to cook a ham one Thanksgiving eve, when Ashley interrupted the lesson with a question. She asked, "Ma, why do you cut the ends off of the ham before you put in the oven?" Tonya replied, "I don't know why, but that's how my mother taught me. Let's call your grandma and ask her."

The grandmother, Carolyn, didn't have a clue as to why the ends of the ham must be cut off before baking, all she knew is that was how it had been done ever since she could remember. That was simply how her mother taught her.

Carolyn put everyone on speakerphone, went to the back room, and asked her mother, Betty, who replied in a shaky voice, "Baby, I cut the ends off the ham because I never had a pan big enough to fit a whole ham."

This is exactly the way the rearing of young boys has taken place in this country, as a matter of the natural course of raising a boy. It continues to this very day!

Instilling the idea that the boy's role does not include the protection or care of women was essential in combating the innate drive which all males of any species possess: tending to the female. After all, the owner fed, clothed, and housed the women.

The black man wasn't needed to provide. The woman worked 16 hours a day just as the man did and neither brought home a dime. The man wasn't needed for the income. So, it seemed to go right along with the program to teach the boys that they were not needed in any responsible way.

If the difference between a man and a boy boils down to what level of responsibility each holds, then it is very difficult for a boy to leave boyhood at all; and you wonder why 30-something-year-old brothers still play with PlayStation and Xbox games. A man was a companion to the woman in those times. He was her consoler, her lover, her friend, her baby maker; but he was not her man. The slave owner did that job for him. The Black man had to provide nothing, earn nothing, and had little interest when his woman struggled against the system, which at the time were the plantation and its owners. Is this not familiar? Does this not reflect, largely, the current state of affairs? Have you seen this scenario played out in your life? Is this still happening in your life?

For a moment, think of your family. How many siblings do you have? How many close cousins? Now think of how many are men and how many are women. Of the women, think of how many have their own apartment or home, a job or career, a car or SUV, good credit or plenty of money to bypass credit.

Likewise, think of how many of your male relatives live with their mamma, girlfriend or baby mamma, have a lousy job or a "hustle," have a piece of car or drives hers, and have jacked-up credit and no checking nor savings accounts. We know who goes to jail, plays video games, doesn't finish school, and smokes weed like its afternoon tea.

No really... pause for a minute. Stop reading and think of your own family members. I'm not trying to dog my brothers, but I'm just being honest. This isn't the case across the board, but you know from your own life that this is real for many.

Our girls have been raised and trained to produce the best lives for themselves and their children under terrible conditions. Our boys have be nurtured and protected against these very same conditions. Instead of using training and skills in life, these brothers are just alive!

Of course, these Black men have hopes and dreams, but they have been ill prepared to achieve them. They, instead, resort to the fantasy of the Hip Hop world, take jobs that offer less than their potential deserves, dive head first into the marginal economy (dealing drugs), or drink and drug to escape the reality of unfulfilled desires.

For the man who marries young or, more often, has children young, the Black woman often finds herself raising a grown boy who has been nurtured by his mother. Often, this grown boy's woman is the one who urges him to get an education and teaches him money management, time management and personal interaction skills.

The problem is that this grown boy's learning curve may be a little more than the woman can handle, and her teaching methods become harsh because she feels he should know this already since she does. (Obviously, she hasn't read this book.) The grown boy is ousted from the relationship just as he is coming to understand what his woman is trying to do for him.

Consequently, the second woman of significance in his life usually has a "real" man, because the first woman finished the job his mother did not complete. This is why so many happily-married husbands and fathers have children from previous relationships.

Many times, our fathers fall into this category of men: men who have not yet cast off the conditioning process that has shaped their minds for hundreds of years. Our fathers may not have been there for us in the capacity of a man. Now you can think it through and understand why. Now you can begin to think about how your mother was stronger than your father. You may think of him without feeling a sense of blind resentment or a blind anger. You may still feel resentful or angry, but it will no longer be blind.

Now you can begin to see your way through relationships with the men in your life. You can begin to forgive them. In forgiving, you free yourself to be loved.

I'm not giving excuses for Black men to be anything other than the very best they can be. What I am offering instead is insight. I'm illustrating the root of a situation that is depressing, destructive, and overly demanding on our women. I am broadening your understanding of the men in your life, so that you may deal with them with empathy.

Hundreds of times in countless conversations, I have heard how women "don't know what's wrong with these Black men out here." Well, now you know! Now you can understand with what you're dealing. Now you can do something about it!

Cool Pose

Majors and Billson coined a phrase called "cool pose," which explains a behavior that African American men adopt as a coping mechanism. Because of the pressure of social, political, and material repression on Black men, a mechanism of protecting their psychological well-being, as black women have for their physical well-being, was engendered.

The cool pose comprises attitudes and behaviors that present a young man as "calm, emotionless, fearless, aloof, and tough." Young men intend this facade to deliver a message of control in the face of adversity and seemingly insurmountable obstacles.

The cool pose suggests competence, high self-esteem, control, and inner strength; it hides the self-doubt, insecurity, and inner turmoil that all humans endure from time to time. This pose often manifests itself in reluctance to show weakness or to communicate emotions, especially the softer forms of communication such as adoration, endearing words, and openly displaying affection. Such a pose may also encourage "tough" behaviors, such as failure to visit doctors, and make it difficult to express warmth and caring in intimate relationships or to negotiate peaceful resolution of conflicts.

Tough behaviors, encouraged by the cool pose, certainly contribute toward young men's rates of violence, suicide, substance abuse, opportunistic infection, and unplanned fatherhood.

This method of self-preservation was designed, over time, to keep the pressure of living in a society that hates Black men from destroying their self-worth. Instead of falling headlong into the pit of despair or derangement, some men decided not to give a damn. They decided since they were not allowed to participate fully in society, they did not have to be concerned with society's moral compass or "typical-folk" tradition.

Their language did not follow conventions of English or Ebonics. They didn't seem particularly concerned with the world at large nor their immediate environment.

When used in context, a word that sums up cool pose nicely and was adopted first by black women, then by popular culture, but originated with black men is "whatever." This phrase is indicative of the attitude used as a barrier against assaults on the personhood of a man. When used in place of an answer, "whatever" has immense power of dissuasion. It causes the person asking questions to back off or give up.

A good example of this attitude which you may or may not have witnessed is when police are handling some incident or altercation where a crowd is assembled, and they ask a black man to stand back or be taken to jail. There is one who says as loudly as possible, "Take me to jail mother_ _ _ _!" Cool pose, in this case, is used as if it will disarm the officer of his main weapon – force.

What It All Means

What it all means is that there are grown men behaving as boys without any awareness at all! It means that there are men walking around without a sense of economic conservation, empathy, or even a real sense of self-responsibility without it being forced upon them. It means that our children have a partial representation of what a man can be, should be, or is. If it weren't for the mothers filling in the gaps of their men's shortcomings, the children would find weak-ass imitations of men living in their home. Well, at least the daughter would, because the son would be raised in exactly the same way and would probably not even notice.

It means that there are ample opportunities for bad decision making. It means that there is a good chance that he won't or can't pay his bills and maintain his credit rating. It means that he can seek out opportunities to betray the trust of his significant other by sharing parts of his body and spirit that he no longer has the right to – parts that he shares with the one whom he claims to love.

What it all means is that there is a great disconnect between manhood and what Black men have been trained to be. Without a sense of empathy, responsibility, and conservation these "men" are merely grown boys. It means exactly what we all know too well – WE ARE IN TROUBLE.

Your Father Had a Dental Plan

Now that we can recognize some of the effects of the survival strategies employed to protect men from harm during slavery, we think back to our fathers and grandfathers and compare the two. We wonder how this unwitting emasculinization did not affect the older generation in the way it has today's men.

The men of the past seem to have courted, dated, married, and stayed home to handle their business. The Black men of today do so much less today than they did two generations ago. I do not think the effects of slavery have a more pronounced effect on today's black men than those from prior generations, but there are other factors to explore that may have been the catalyst for the current absence of men leading Black homes.

Black Men:

I believe the combination of the psychological processes that were employed to reduce a black man's effectiveness in dealing with society and the economic and social impact of the loss of the manufacturing sector was the beginning of the end for two-parent Black households as the norm. The blossoming of women, Black and white, in educational and career attainment could not have been timed more poorly for the plight of the Black family. It came at the junction of the end of segregation, the beginning of the collapse of the industrial sector, and the middle Civil Rights struggle.

Although these events, with the exception of the collapse of industry, are viewed by many as breakthroughs for American society, they have had negative impact on Black families - effects which have not been thoroughly examined to date.

There has been research on the negative effects of the Civil Rights movement and integration on lives of Black Americans, including books that explore the disastrous effects of integration on the education of Black children. As with education, there have been significant problems introduced by integration in the loss of an independent Black economy and Black women's move from working as domestics to working in corporate America. No one can debate that these achievements meant great progress for African Americans, but they did have their share of drawbacks.

We can also understand the perspectives of the women with whom these men partnered and raised families. Quite often, the women of our mother's and grandmother's generations tell of a version of marriage quite different than what they have related to their children. They speak of the reality of living in loveless marriages out of economic necessity and cultural expectations or of feeling trapped with the responsibility of raising children and their men early on in the relationships – something today's women no longer have to endure.

Black Men:

From the 1950s to as recently as 2010, the opportunities for Black men to have gainful employment that included living wages, good benefits, and promotion potential have disappeared as a result of the decline in the manufacturing of steel products, automobiles, televisions, appliances, textiles, and furniture. More than 42,000 factories have closed in the U.S. since 2000 alone and have been shipped to Latin America and Asia. This number does not even begin to reflect the loss of factory and plant jobs during the 40 years prior.

If you notice, the loss of this part of American industry occurred at exactly the same period as the loss of the Black father. This alone doesn't account for the mass fleeing of responsible fathers, as demonstrated by the example of white men who abandoned their families at a much lower rate. But with the mindset of immaturity and irresponsibility deeply imbedded in their psyche and the "first fired" reality of racist America, factory closures did a great deal to intensify the mass flight of Black fathers.

Without factory jobs and the stability they provided, Black men became either underemployed or unemployed in large numbers. The options open to a person without a college education or the mindset to even pursue college education came in the form of service and support oriented jobs that offered low or minimum wages, no benefits, and no real chance for promotion into management – in short, dead-end jobs. This involuntary forcing of Black men into the underemployed or unemployment ranks is known as institutional deprivation.

Institutional deprivation meant that men had to retreat into the shadowy world of bootlegging, numbers running, drug dealing, and theft in order to survive. This criminal activity led to the wholesale incarceration of millions of these men – men who would normally make an honest living. This mass jailing is also a part of what we now know as institutional decimation and continues to leech from the pool of available Black husbands. It produces a third class citizen that lives perpetually with the scarlet letter of a criminal record, thereby severely reducing even the slimmest options for employment as an unskilled laborer.

Ironically, just as the Black man began to find his place in America becoming one of poverty and long-odds chances for success, the Black woman was moving forward in personal and political clout. Riding the wave of the civil rights movement and the resulting legislation, Black women found the world of education and work welcoming and receptive to their desires to move forward. Be clear, however, that it wasn't the racial equality laws from the movement that provided opportunity; it was the use of these laws by white women to fuel the feminist agenda that provided the great benefit.

Taking into account the dwindling number of upwardly mobile Black men and the ever-increasing number of Black women being educated and integrated into the workplace, an imbalance in the household economy is apparent. This restructured the traditional roles of provider and nurturer. With the woman earning wages and salaries that far exceeded those of her partner, the often missing male-leader characteristics, and the resentment that comes with the role reversal; it is no wonder that millions of potential relationships became problematic rather than progressive.

Even for those not outpacing Black men in the workplace, there is still the problem of institutional subsidization that suppresses the reliance on Black men in an even more insidious manner. Where a man is not being out-earned or out-learned, the woman he is with may rely on him for assistance. If she is impoverished and is in need of a job opportunity, the state and federal governments supply her with all the basics she needs to survive – food, shelter, and healthcare.

Black Men:

This is the same dynamic from the chapter on Black men, only now no one lives in the slave owner's backyard. Instead, they live on the government's property or a government lease known as the section eight program

No longer would Black women need men to financially care for them or their children. They would not need to deal with the irresponsible attributes that were taught to their husbands as children. This came at a time when the men were losing the ability to fully provide for their families – and the results have been disastrous.

Blacks Earning College Degrees[1]

- Black women outnumber their male counterparts by 27%

- 68% of Black men who start college do not graduate within six years, which is the lowest college completion rate among any group

- In 1980 Black males comprised 44% of all Blacks enrolled in higher education

- In 2007 Black males were 35% of all Blacks enrolled in higher education

---

[1] U.S. Department of Education

Black Men:

Fig 1. African American Degrees Earned by Type

Degree	Men	Women
Bachelor's	34%	66%
Master's	28%	72%
1st Professional	37%	63%
Doctoral	44%	66%

Between 1997 and 2007, black women INCREASED the number of college degrees earned, while Black men stayed constant.

The Down Low Myth

Everyone in the Black community knows of the phrase "down low brother." This is the language used to describe a Black man that lives the life of a gay man in private while pretending to be straight in public. The mainstream term "in the closet" has been replaced with "down low," a phrase taken from the hip hop popular culture defined as being discreet to the point of absolute secrecy.

Race doesn't dictate the amount of homosexuality in a population, culture does. By this, I mean the difference between the numbers of openly gay men in any community is related more to the individual's cultural affiliation than to genetic differences between the so-called races, because there is no genetic difference. It is the difference in culture that persuades Black men to hide their sexuality more so than is done in mainstream culture because of the sense of repulsion for the lifestyle. Discovering that a man is homosexual is a much bigger deal in Black culture.

Unequally Yoked (2 Corinthians 6:14)

It is no mystery that the African American man is out paced by the African American woman. Perhaps the most telling figure is the high school graduation rate which is an indicator of the most basic educational achievement. It was 46% for African American men and 60% for African American women in 2007.

This creates an obvious imbalance in financial mobility which affects one's ability to obtain material objects of equal quality, travel with equal freedom, live in equal housing, and provide equal food, clothing, and education for one's children. Many pastors speak of these examples when speaking of "unequally yoked." (2 Corinthians 6:14)

I think of the example of being yoked as cattle are is misleading, at best, and perhaps insulting, given the history of our use as farm "animals". A yoke is a wooden or leather harness that connects cattle or horses, then called draft animals, at the shoulder. Typically, the animals are of the same size and strength, therefore they are able to pull similar sized carts or wagons at similar speeds and for similar distances. The progress made by the carts or wagons can be measured and anticipated with some consistency.

The trouble with the draft animal analogy is that, unlike human beings, these animals cannot change their ability to pull the car. They cannot grow larger or stronger if they decide. Human beings, in this case black men, can grow in size and strength - figuratively of course. Unlike a draft animal, a man can get more education, earn more money, or get a better job.

The One Dimensional Brother

If you were to search through your own life and the men in it, you would notice that you may have friends, family or someone you have dated who are one-dimensional in nature. I find that there are two types of one-dimensional Black men. These two types are: the sex brother and the money brother.

Keep in mind that, although there are other, smaller dimensions to these individuals besides, their most dominant dimension overshadows and makes useless the other facets of their personality. Beware of these two types:

The Sex Brother

The sex brother thinks in terms of sex. He goes to bed thinking of sex, and he wakes up thinking the same. He's at work thinking of sex, and he drives home thinking of sex. When he shops he thinks of sex, and when he is pumping gas he thinks of sex. He gets a good education to get a good woman. Not a good woman for marriage, but a woman with a good body that he considers good for sex. He gets a good job to get more sex.

All his thoughts, and subsequently his actions, are based, at their core, in the pursuit of sex. He exists in a pornographic reality where the basic theme of life is to obtain sex. He is like one giant penis. This is the brother that women speak of when they call men dogs. Ironically, this is not far from the truth, as they hump around sleeping with any woman they can convince to have sex with them.

The Money Brother

The money brother believes life revolves around money - chasing it, getting it, spending it, showing it, and relishing in the security that it brings. Everything he has done thus far in life has been in the pursuit of money and all things that can be obtained with it.

He may have said that he wants the best education to attain some sense of achievement, but in reality, he wants the best education to earn the most money. If he is a businessman, he may have said that he became an entrepreneur for the freedom of having no boss, but this is usually not the case. He became an entrepreneur to generate the most money possible for his time and effort.

The money brother loves to show off his money, whether it is a new set of gold teeth or a new Gulfstream. These brothers range from the local drug peddler on the street corner to the syndicated television evangelist that drives his Bentley to Neiman Marcus on Saturday and preaches prosperity while collecting his "tithes" on Sunday.

Understanding the Black Man

Understanding the Black Woman

Throughout our history in this country, the woman has been the central figure in the African American community. From Slavery to the present, the African American woman has been stuck with multiple roles and has developed many survival strategies to maintain our existence as a people. Ironically, these strategies ensure that our relationships don't work.

These survival strategies were developed so that the Black woman could successfully navigate the world of the white male. To function in her role in the slave owner's society, she had to operate both as a Black female mother and a white male manager. In her role as a Black woman/white man, she had to develop a sort of multiple personality strategy.

This dual personality had to ensure that she would not be marginalized as a woman the way white men marginalized white women, nor would she be marginalized as a man the way white men marginalized black men. She would instead be to white men, by virtue of her value both physically and symbolically, the second player in the antebellum South.

The prevailing thought even during pre colonial times was that tending farmlands was hard work and was not suited for European women, even as African women "were able to work like the men in the fields." This relegated white women to their traditional roles of tending to food, clothing, and children. The inclusion in the production and generation of wealth gave Black women an advantage of value in the collective minds of those who owned slaves and property, governed society, and influenced social and political norms.

The result is visible even today when you walk through the halls of IBM or Booz Allen; most of the Blacks are women – except in the cafeteria and mailroom. What isn't so visible is the side effect of this transgenerational gender blending as we shall see later.

Entitlement Syndrome

The entitlement syndrome is based upon a concept that individuals function in relationships, to some degree, with the belief that a partner owes what was not provided within the family as they grew up. When this occurs, feelings of entitlement dominate the healthy flow of the relationship, causing frustration and disappointment.

Another variation of this syndrome follows the Adult Fairy Tales taught to Black women by their mothers. They reach adulthood thinking that the world, America, and even Jesus owes them the perfect life because they "did everything they were supposed to do."

Adult Fairy tales

Adult fairy tales, much like children's fairy tales, are stories and allegories that have little or no significant value when building a life or constructing a plan of action in order to accomplish a goal. For example, one of the more prominent tales in the African American community is one told by mothers to their daughters. Mother tells young teenage daughter that if she goes to school, gets a good job, buys a nice car, and buys a nice house; her life will be fine, her life will be great, a man will come along and marry her, and they will have kids. The unstated part of the equation implies that everything will come together.

When we are in this fairy tale part of instruction, there is no advice or guidance on choosing a career, which is often determined by a slight interest in unknown industries and monetary consideration. In many cases, the mother has no idea about a white collar career, corporate America, and may not know what a glass ceiling is, much less have any experience touching it.

In this case, the fairy tale is a lot weaker than it is in the case of college educated mothers doling out the same standard issue bullshit. With these mothers/storytellers the story has much more authenticity and is lent more credibility by the fact that this woman has worked in corporate America, made a lot of money, been married (and possibly divorced), and had children, house, car, etc. She is a veritable expert in this particular tale.

The problem is the tale still rings false because she has endured many years of unhappy relationships, job dissatisfaction, and indescribable feelings of emptiness and loneliness, while yearning for true happiness. She has fulfilled everything that the fairy tale holds to be true in its formula of school, job, house car, (material possessions and the means to acquire them), and yet she goes unfulfilled.

Black Men:

What about the central theme of fairy tales themselves – the moral of the story? The moral of this particular fairy tale is that you'll live happily ever after. Using this formula without going back to review, revise, and revamp your life, you just may find your life lacking.

This fairy tale is based largely on the deep-seated survival strategy of androgynous role play that Black women had to adopt to survive slavery. At a time when Black men were relegated to pure labor, the women had to be engaged with white males in negotiation, discussion, and commerce as representatives for their owners, their family, or themselves. In essence, during this time, white men and Black women were the only persons visible since as white women were de facto property of white men, and Black men were literally property of white men.

Through centuries of engagement between Black women and white men, Black women learned and taught their daughters how to communicate as white men communicate. This meant behaving not only as a white person but, more importantly, as a male. Over time, this androgynous perspective was adapted and gradually became what we now know as the "Black woman with attitude."

Adaptation in the case of this fairy tale comes across in the success strategy itself. The notion of material attainment (financial security) in order to provide for and maintain the household is traditionally a male role function. In other words, ladies, what the hell does having a good education, a good career, making good money, and buying all that stuff have to do with getting married to a good man and having a good family? It is absurd to consider such a strategy for obtaining happiness in the life of a woman, but then again, fairy tales are often absurd, which is why they should always be relegated to fiction.

As a variation on this same tall tale, white mothers instruct their daughters in a similar fashion. Instead of modeling themselves in this androgynous role play, they are taught to be the catch by being in the right place at the right time.

Their tale revolves around the damsel and the prince – the damsel being a college-age white woman leaving her parents' home for an adventure. The damsel's purpose is not to get an economics degree (although she may pick up one along the way), but she is in search of economic stability in the form of a husband.

This is not to say that there aren't those who go to college with purely scholarly intent. The scholarly types just don't tend to see much credibility in fairy tales. They instead tend to be career-driven and, later in life, find difficulty with long-term relationships for other reasons.

For a few reasons the damsel scenario is different from that of a Black woman going to college. Their intent is to catch a man while they're in college – while their physical appearance is at its peak. The cultural expectation is that the college experience ends childhood and begins adulthood, which is also the acceptable point for marriage and starting a family.

The Cost of Being Single

Only 33% of black women and 44% of black men were married in 2007. Although black men and women had higher household income growth than men and women overall, the sharp decline in marriage rates among blacks hindered growth in their incomes. Among black women with high school educations, household incomes actually declined from 1970 to 2007, reflecting a change in the composition of this group from majority married (with the higher incomes that accompany this status) to majority unmarried.

Black Men:

White women often go to college, meet potential spouses and their families, and, with good luck, are engaged and marry soon after entering the work force. This produces early economic advantages for both the man and woman as they have one household with double the income and half the expenses.

This allows the couple to save, invest, and grow their money. For example, two new college graduates recently married start off with a small nest egg of wedding gift cash. Let us say they both start with $50,000 salaries and they rent an apartment at $1,000 per month.

Married v. Unmarried

Married 25 year old couple:
- $18,000/year = rent and utilities
- $60,000 net income/year
- 200 wedding guests might net you $10,000
- $42,000 disposable income (savings, investments, insurance, etc.)

Single 25 year old woman:
- $14,000/year = rent and utilities
- $30,000 net income/year
- No Wedding Money
- $16,000 disposable income (savings, investments, insurance, etc.)

10 Years Later

The married couple potentially has $250,000 or more that they have either saved or invested. The husband and wife are now ready to start a family. They are ready to buy their first home having invested and used their wedding gift money and the interest earned from it for the down payment. Instantly, their assets have gone up. They have a $250,000 home and $250,000 in the bank. They have assets to leverage everything else in their lives. They start their family off on much firmer footing than if they were single.

This single woman is now 35, and her savings is probably much less than the married couple. Then she decides to marry at 35 instead of 25.

Very different scenarios are created off the bat. Because all the material success was gained together as a couple, it makes their lives more intertwined and there's less incentive for them to split up. What is theirs is truly theirs and not his or hers. They built a financial life together that strengthens their bond.

The woman who marries at 35 comes into the marriage with "hers," and the husband comes into the marriage with "his." Together, they try to make it "theirs." In spite of all their efforts to develop what's "theirs," there is still the presence of things obtained separately.

Not only does this separation not act to strengthen the ties between them in a way the couple married out of college is strengthened, but it may also cause issues with the remaining independent material identities. During times when the relationship is stressed or threatened, it is easy to fall back on how well you were doing without the other person. Then, you remember how much you really didn't need the other person in the first place. When these two get married, they don't develop like the other couple. Without significant growth they do not bring 100% to the table. They don't catch up to the other couple financially.

Black women employ this fairy tale-based strategy while totally ignoring the biological factors involved with having a family. By that, I mean their physical appearance wanes as they get older, and their ability to get a man is diminished. Plus, even as they exercise religiously to preserve the appearance of youth, their uterus and eggs are getting older, which puts them in a position of having potentially less healthy children and/or risky childbirth scenarios.

The divorce of a couple with older kids has less traumatic effect on the children than if those children were younger. An older person with a young child is less likely to get remarried than a younger person with an older child. Men aren't big on other people's kids either, so the older they are the less responsibility that man has.

In the androgyny model, the Black woman does what a white man does – goes to college, builds a career, builds a home, and then tries to build a relationship and a family. This occurs 10 to 15 years after her white counterparts who have been living with half the bills and double the income just by being married. It seems that one gets further ahead by getting married early than by trying to get ahead financially.

A 35 year old woman and 21 year old woman are sometimes very different physically in the eyes of a man seeking to start a family. Unfortunately, many Black women, such as the 35 year old, often 'career' themselves out of compatible options for spouses.

Be Agreeable

Black women have had many stereotypes heaped upon them over the years, but the most, and perhaps the closest to reality, is the black woman's bad attitude.

The media has picked up on this theme of the mouthy sister who appears literally ready to pounce on any would be trash talker, advantage taker, or general offender that dare make the mistake of bringing any of it her way. The media now uses it liberally to color the characters they develop for their TV programs and feature films.

It was nothing out of the ordinary to see Dr. Bailey from Grey's Anatomy displaying police officer behavior, but instead of guns, mace, and handcuffs, she is armed with a smart mouth, quick wit, and a fearlessness that frightens most. I contend this behavior is one of the more detrimental vestiges of slavery that lies at the core of our relationship issues. The fact of the matter is that men do not want to be contested by women at every turn.

Men have a natural inclination to lead. This inclination to lead requires someone to follow - a woman. It is like the principle of yin-yang - with the woman being the yin, the force of continuity and stability that keeps the processes of life and situations in motion and the man being the yang, the dynamic force that applies action to life and situations – the catalyst.

It seems the behaviors of Black women are more in line with the behaviors of all men, and this is in accord with the problem. If there are two dynamic, action forces (yang) within one relationship, then there are two methods, styles, and means of action. They may run contrary to one another, thus forestalling all action and creating no momentum at all. Further, it leaves no one to bring to bear the force of continuity which is needed to maintain the longevity of the relationship. Without the principle of "following the action plan", the result is no movement and no progress in the relationship.

This is why relationships with many powerful couples tend to end rather quickly. There are typically two action (yang) forces at work and very little continuity at work. Celebrities are notorious for being hard-driving and action oriented thus out of sync with the yin-yang type of unity.

Black Men:

This behavior that is common to black women and powerful individuals of any race comes from learning to navigate in a white man's world by emulating his behavior. White women sometimes do this consciously, as in the cases of Martha Stewart, and Madonna. Black women do this unconsciously, as a result of what I call Generational Masculinization.

Thinking about the problem of behaving with male communication styles is easy – but what about solutions? The solution to this issue is rather simple but may be more difficult to adapt in your everyday life. Just be agreeable. It is as simple as that.

The act of being agreeable as your baseline attitude, as opposed to being mired in male behaviorisms, opens more avenues of communication than can be imagined. Being agreeable means a person has an open mind and can listen to the opinions of others without assuming there are some motivations by the speaker to take advantage.

Listen to everyone and anyone without expecting anything. Listen to what they say without adding any additional meaning to their words. The same goes for strangers. Give everyone the benefit of the doubt. It will open up a new world of communication and cooperation from which you can truly get what you want without the conflict-induced force you have adopted from white men and used as a negotiation tool for so long.

Black Men:

Racial Differences in Human Sexuality

The differences between our cultural origins give us conflicting ways of dealing with relationships, marriage, and family. European culture has its origins in the last ice age. African-descended people have cultural origins in the tropical climate of the Nile Valley in East Africa.

The differences of our cultural origins (African) and our current cultural environment (European) give us conflicting ways of dealing with God, family, money, and most importantly, the opposite sex.

This Nile valley culture became the cultural patterns of African people in general, and during the slave trade, these patterns, including marriage and family patterns practiced for millennia, accompanied the enslaved Africans to the Western hemisphere. Even as African Americans had to adapt and assimilate to the European marriage and courtship practices, they also retained, consciously and unconsciously, their African patterns and practices.

Concerning marriage and courtship, the differences between the two cultures extend into the family structure and affect many aspects of communication, values, and loyalties. Whereas the western (European) marriage redefines the "who" and "what" is most important in the family from the day the couple's vows are taken, the African marriage retains the family order from which the husband and wife came. The woman in the marriage becomes the wife first and the daughter, sister, and aunt second in the western cultural pattern. The European woman marries and the rest of the family becomes "second" to their new pair bond and their children, remaining most loyal to her husband.

In the African pattern, she remains most loyal to her family first, and then her husband is "added" into her family as a secondary relative –

as she does into his also. Whereas the European couple "starts" a family, the African couple "joins" a family.

The African, and now African American, family structure is based around many relatives that are considered "close" family even if they are cousins, aunts, and uncles – often having no real distinction from siblings in their relationships. Even when family does not live in close proximity, they retain the concept and order of their relationships and often rely on one another for financial and emotional support for each other, each other's children, the elderly, and the sick. This is known as the consanguineous relationship, or "blood ties."

Because of the significance of the consanguineous tie, the nuclear family built around the husband, wife and children is not the primary family structure for African Americans. For many, the marriage does not replace other primary relationships - the mother-daughter relationship or the mother-son relationship, for example.

So when thinking of family stability in the Black household, there are clear distinctions between the married couple and the family. This is not to say that marriage is not highly valued, as it is considered a life-long union. It does imply that the nuclear family is not the primary point of kinship it is in European culture.

With the expectation learned from living within European culture, the man expects the woman to cleave from her parents and family to make him the center of her focus. While she expects the same, and although these expectations are considered the "norm", it is not what their primary culture has taught them is the standard. When one has competing ideas as in this case, cognitive dissonance is the result. Cognitive dissonance is anxiety that results from simultaneously holding contradictory or otherwise incompatible attitudes, beliefs, or ideas about the same subject. The outward expression is tension that seeks to be resolved and is often dealt with, unconsciously, in self-destructive behaviors.

Even more important than the ways in which family deals with marriage from culture to culture are the differences in which family structures are formed. European culture origins were adapted during the Würm glaciations or what we call the last ice age. During this time Western Europe was cold, wet and in many places covered in vast sheets of ice not unlike that found in Antarctica today.

Fruit and crops don't grow in the cold and icy climates and small animals were not widely found. The animals one could find were large and dangerous and often preyed on human beings. Adaptations to this food scarcity and environmental threats from animals created a culture that is more violent, aggressive, and xenophobic.

Black Men:

The lack of food creates an environment in which predators and other human beings may kill for one's food or kill one FOR food. Adapting social behaviors in order to cope with such harsh conditions meant that the European people became tough, hard-spirited, life and death-centric and able to kill without remorse.

Over thousands of years the weather also created physical adaptations that aligned with scarce food sources. Lower birth rates through less fertility means fewer mouths to feed. Social patterns that send the elderly off into the wilderness on their "last walk" means not feeding those that are not productive.

These conditions of scarcity gave rise to the nuclear family. The nuclear family means that there are as few mouths to feed as possible. This is contrary to other cultures in which the communal life is the norm.

Whether it is South Asian, African, or South American, culture that initially developed in tropical or subtropical climates tend to have many wives and many children. Cousins, aunts, and uncles are considered an integral part of the family unlike their roles within European and northern Asian cultures where today they only see each other during the holidays.

The simple reason these cultures of the Southern Hemisphere have large families and many wives is as simple as the reason why Europe and Northern Asia do not – climate. Whereas the last ice age made food scarce and nature cruel, the tropical and sub-tropical climates made small game, fruit, vegetables, and warmth a year-round occurrence. There was no shortage to speak of and everyone ate well and felt no threat because of it.

What was plentiful was easily shared and the communal form of living was born. Elders were not relied upon for production so they were not sent off into the wilderness to die. To this day the major difference in how we care for our elders is the same. Blacks tend to keep the elder in the home of the child with the most affinity toward caring for the health and other issues that come with getting older. Europeans, on the other hand, no longer send their aging parents to the wilderness but instead send them to senior homes.

This harsh climate also affected the development of religious philosophy. God was not thought of as a vengeful and jealous being that smites the Earth and drives famine and disease in the South as they had perceived in the North. God was a benevolent God with many attributes that symbolically pointed toward being fruitful and building large families and being thankful for the bounty on receives. Challenges in life were recognized not as punishment, but as learning experiences.

This idea that a man has many children with many women is tens of thousands of years old; it cannot and did not change in the relatively brief 400 years we have been living as pseudo Europeans. Think of the older Black man's funeral when ALL of his children gather, many never having met one another. For that matter think of your father, brother, or uncle – they may have more than one mother of their children.

Just like the strategies of survival during slavery that are embedded into elements of our behaviors, the ways in which we gather, share meals, or celebrate holidays are based on African culture hidden within what we sense as our normal behavior, our particular version of Western culture or "being Black". Harems and the tradition of many wives that we associate with African culture are acceptable when the cultural "rules" allow, in America we just do it anyway.

We often have a sense of shame that follows the cognitive dissonance created by living a life of what W.E.B. DuBois called the "twoness" of being Black in America. Man-sharing in the Southern cultural norm and monogamy from the Western cultural norm compete for the mental "space" of what is right and wrong when it comes to polygamy.

A Woman's Worth

This difference in family politics is not the only contrast in the two cultures that has been merged into the African American way of relating in family. The difference in the roles of family politics is also reflected in the way gender is viewed and assigned.

White Americans value gender very differently from African Americans and the fact that Blacks use both viewpoints leads us into destructive relationships. The cultural patterns of African Americans are a mixture of both modern European culture and the African traditional culture that has survived slavery.

In traditional European culture, women are typically resigned to roles of preparing and serving the food, weaving clothing, and raising and educating the children. Women are viewed as the center of family in traditional African culture, even as the man is the primary participant in politics, war, and consensus decision-making. From the European perspective, these roles stand as the leadership in society, but in the African viewpoint, they are but maintenance functions of secondary importance to the continuity of the families within the society. It is the family that holds the most value and it is led by women – having husbands as figureheads to represent these interests publicly.

This still holds true today within Black families but with the influence and pressure of modern Western family gender roles intertwined in often concealed and conflicting ways. The combination of this dynamic and the "blended gender" effects from slave survival strategies create an enormous amount of confusion in the expectations of African American couples. The

Black Men:

degree of confusion and conflict may vary from family to family.

7 Steps To Change a Black Man's Life

This book may not attract as many male readers and particularly not those that might benefit from the following advice, so I give it to you as sister, girlfriend, wife, mother, cousin, and friend. If in any way you see the need to impart any or this entire seven step plan in the life of a man, teen, or boy in your life, do so. By suggestion, guile, force, coercion, or duress, whatever it takes do it because it is THAT important.

Do Something!

Do anything! Just do something! One major issue confronting African American men is their being content with dreaming of a better life, but not doing anything about it. It is this kind of complacent mentality that gives time permission to let the months and years roll by without accomplishment, satisfaction or growth occurring in his life. It is as if he waits for a knock at the door from some guy named "Opportunity!"

So, I say DO SOMETHING! Go to school, get a job, read a book, volunteer at a homeless shelter, or go for a walk every day. Do anything that will get you moving and some blood circulating through your brain and body. Take a break from the weed, the beer, the TV, and give your Xbox/PS3/or whatever to your child, niece, nephew, or little cousin of your choice. Xboxes are good for, children and independently wealthy people; both of which have hours to waste staring at an inanimate object.

Getting yourself moving is the idea, and if you think about it, you should have never stopped moving in the first place. Once, you were active and excited about living. You played sports, went to school, and you were alive. Nowadays, you are too cool to work at a job that pays at the unskilled labor rate, even though you have no skills. Get a job . . . then get some skills . . . then get an education . . . and then the house . . . and car . . . and beautiful woman . . . in short, get a life!

7 Steps to Change Your Life

STEP 1 – Get an idea of how you are going to make it out of your current life and into your new life

Don't just fantasize about some vague idea of driving a Benz or Bentley or living the life of a "baller." In clear and concise words and images, think of what you will do to produce the ingredients needed for such material things. How much does it cost? Where would I get it? What generates the kind of money needed to get those things? How do I fit in with the activities that generate that king of income?

From there, figure how long it should take you and what progress you should see along the way. What should I do or change by tomorrow, next week, next month, next year, etc.?. You will then know how to adjust to get to your goal.

Think in the same way about your relationships. Get all debt, old grudges, and resentments into the open and out of your life. Pay them back, call them up, forgive them, and forget them. Get on good terms with your family by simply calling them. You do not need a reason to call, just let them put you on their mind – let them wonder about you because it will give you great positive energy in the near future as you put your plan to work.

STEP 2 – Get stable and consistent

Get a routine going in your life once you get up and moving. Make a list of things to do every day at the same time. It does not matter what it is, just get in the habit of getting up and going everyday so that you become conditioned to the 'Mother of Learning" and an important ingredient for success – repetition.

The Grand Canyon was formed by a small river that ran through it day after day and year after year until it was worn clean through. Bodybuilders workout every day in order to turn their bodies into living statues the same way professional athletes practice every day to become the best in the world at their respective sports.

STEP 3 – Talk to someone

Have a sincere conversation with someone that has his or her act together. Talk about what they do and how they do it. Forget about being embarrassed, many successful men and women would love to tell you how they made their way to success. Listen to them and apply their strategies to your own game plan. Whatever it is that you want to do, do it, but follow the steps taken by those who have reached their goals or are well on their way.

STEP 4 – Make a pledge

Make a pledge to take care of your responsibility, and then do what you say you will do. Your kids, your credit, your weight, that dream or passion that God put in your heart – anything that you know you should be doing, make a decision to do it.

STEP 5 – Get connected

Make phone calls, do research, and ask questions. Do whatever you must in order to make contacts. Being connected is essential to changing your life and building a meaningful bridge to the world of movers and shakers. There is someone, somewhere waiting to help you do what it is you want to do your goals – just know what when you approach.

STEP 6 – Execute your plan

Motivate yourself. Get the images of how you want to live out of your head and put them in front of your eyes. Surround yourself with the feelings and thoughts of how you want to live your life. This means placing pictures on your wall, writing notes to yourself, noticing things you see on a daily basis that remind you of the material things you want and the kind of people you need or want in your life. Notice the feelings that others show on their faces and in their actions. Notice them and what they do when no one is looking.

Keep track of your progress. Keep a list of things you must do to get to the lifestyle you want to have. Most importantly, use your imagination to visualize yourself in your new life, driving your new car, with your new woman, parking in the driveway of your new luxury home.

STEP 7 – Cleanse yourself

Brainwash yourself. By this, I am not advising you to go out and join a cult or buy a book on self-hypnosis. I am advising you to wash your brain, figuratively, of course! Wash your brain of all things negative and untrue. Remove all ideas about what you have been doing and how it will get you to where you want to be by some magical process.

The magic is in believing you can accomplish what you will and taking some action – any action. A lot of us loudly proclaim our excellence, and quietly doubt that our lives will be as bright as we say. This way of thinking must be washed away immediately! It is the surest way, over time, to rob you of that fire called a will and its fuel called desire.

Will –power allows men to do whatever their hearts desire. It puts you in a position to exercise your choice of actions without worrying about whether or not you will fail. This is so because the will does not know failure, nor does it comprehend setbacks. The will only seeks to complete the task and fulfill the desired outcome. It cares less about anything else. This single-minded focus creates for men whatever they will.

Black Men:

7 Steps To Change a Black Woman's Love Life

Every single relationship you have is a reflection of how you feel about yourself. You are a magnet attracting all things via the signals you emit via your thoughts and feelings. Every relationship you have and every interaction with every person is a reflection of your own thoughts and feelings at that very moment. To get the man you want in your life and any other relationship for that matter, you must fall in love with you! You must love yourself deeply and honestly.

This message of "loving yourself" is the mantra we hear all the time, but usually without an explanation of what it means or how to achieve it. I propose that loving yourself is like loving someone else – accepting them as they are. Accepting yourself as you are is a matter of knowing what you like and dislike about yourself, and then changing what you can and accepting what you can't.

Think about the people you love and those characteristics they have which you could do without. Since you know you can't change them, you just accept them and love them anyway. This unconditional love is what you must have for yourself, but since it is you, there is an option to love yourself even more and make changes if you like, something you cannot expect from others.

You probably know what about you is likable and what is not. The behaviors and attitudes you have that you would rather do without are probably noticeable to others as well. If these attitudes and behaviors can be changed, change them. If they cannot be changed, accept them. This is the beginning of loving yourself even greater.

Many sources say that you must accept everything about yourself, flaws and all. I say that this is the lazy way out and is based on a philosophy that encourages mediocrity and discourages growth in all areas of life – work, health, and relationships included. I say take the "eff it!" approach and choose to accept, change, and improve who you have been, who you are, and who will become. This, of course, requires more than just accepting that EVERYTHING about yourself is okay, and it is a very important step in bringing loving relationships into your life.

If you think about it, what in life that is worth having comes easily? Childbirth, going to school, advancing in your career, or writing a book are all difficult endeavors that bring with them a lifetime of rich rewards. Why not put in as much work to attain a lifetime of love?

If you are fat and don't like being fat, then the people around you will know that you are not comfortable being fat. They, too, become uncomfortable with it, and it becomes an issue they would rather not have. Not that being fat is something people dislike about their friends; it is the discomfort they feel from you that becomes associated, in their minds, with you being fat.

Whether you are aware of it or not, it holds true that anything you dislike about yourself others will dislike also. This is as good a reason to want to change as any, because not only will you remove discomfort from your friends and potential mates, but you will also remove discomfort from yourself.

So, lose that weight if it bothers you! Drop the bad attitude if you know you have one! Be more outgoing if you feel you are too reserved! Do whatever it is you want to do to love yourself and your ways even more than you love them now! This is a key to garnering greater love from those who love you now and those who will love you in the future.

As for what you cannot change, you must accept. Accept the past, especially. The past is what shapes your concept - who you think you are, whether it is accurate or not.

We often reference the past to shape excuses for our current shortcomings, flaws, and disappointments. We have bought into what popular psychology touts and I call the "therapy model." The "therapy model" leads one to believe that the current version of yourself is nothing but a result of your past experiences, and it deals more with the flaws and pathologies of life than the successes and achievements.

The thinking is that success comes from hard work, luck, and good genes and not some specific incident or event from your remote past. This idea removes the past as an attribute to use for moving forward, but it encourages the idea that limitations in your life are excused by something that you cannot change (the past) and therefore may limit your life forever. This thinking is WRONG!

Eff It!

I say forget the therapy model and learn to say and think 'eff it!' (Fuck it!) and move on to being whatever you decide you want to be. The eff it approach clears away all the past and present roadblocks to making you the most loveable you that you can be. It is truly an exercise in freedom to just say "fuck it" and do whatever you will.

Saying to yourself "eff it" is the essence of worry-free living and it can be summed up with these seven phrases:

STEP 1 – Fuck it!

Dismiss worry, guilt, anxiety, etc. by revealing what they really are - fear.

STEP 2 – Forget it

Understand that the past is but a memory – it cannot be changed, redone, or deleted. It can, however be forgotten.

STEP 3 – Fix it

Remember we all make mistakes, but seldom do we find the courage or humility to return to the mistake and make it right. This is a very powerful step and often does more than mend the mistake.

STEP 4 – Fight it

Fight off the ills, addictions, and habits we all have which often rob us of happiness or peace of mind. Fight them off by not fighting them at all – Eff it!

STEP 5 – Flee it

Remove yourself from anything (and I mean anything) that is making you feel bad. There is no exception to this rule except childbirth and surgery.

STEP 6 – Find it

Determine your path, your place, your passion, your promise, your faith, your legacy, your hobby, your . . .

STEP 7 – Fulfill it

Realize your destiny is what YOU determine it is. There is NOT a destiny prescribed for you, God knows your steps but doesn't take them for you. YOU make your own destiny day-by-day through thought and effort.

From the vantage point of the "eff it" approach, you can see clearly what is easy, possible, or difficult to accomplish. You will be free and clear of all the negative thinking that has hindered you so far in every aspect of life, especially your relationship issues. You will no longer be concerned with them – you will just act on them. When action replaces worry, things get done, progress happens, and satisfaction results.

No longer will you daydream about that fine brother at work, but you will take steps to get him into your life. You won't worry about what MAY happen, because you will control all the outcomes that you can and those you cannot control you won't even think about. You won't worry about what someone thinks of you because you no longer subscribe to "if he only knew how good a woman I am" because you make your true self an outward part of you. You no longer worry about people taking advantage of you because you feel no desire to be timid or at the mercy of others opinions, you know you are being the most authentic person you can be, and if they don't like the real you, then eff it!

With the full acceptance of yourself and understanding what you will change, you feel renewed and confident about the true, and seemingly new, you. You walk through the world knowing you are in command of everything about you, and the past has little bearing on your present and future aside from what you decide to maintain that has helped you succeed thus far.

When you have full control over your thoughts and feelings about yourself, you know that you are all the "you" you can be at that moment and there are no greater expectations, either from others or yourself, that matter.

Believe In Yourself

The most attractive thing men find in a woman over the long haul is her knowing what she wants, who she is, and what she is all about. Sometimes this is offset by a woman's lack of self confidence or her decision to be sold on someone else's dreams and ideas. I say believe in you, your desires for your life and your ability to get them accomplished!

Although it is fine to actively participate in your church, to actively in a prayer life, and to actively worship and honor God in your own way, you should ultimately believe in the greatest gift

God has ever given you - your life and your right mind.

The majority of us truly do not believe in ourselves. We usually believe in a version of ourselves given to us by others. Whether it's your brothers and/or sisters telling you what they think of you out of spite, envy, or jealousy, your boss telling you how he or she sees about you via performance reviews, or even from your significant other who may not think very much of themselves deep down inside, attacking your character, we seldom have an authentic idea of ourselves from our own point of view.

If you were to seriously think of yourself without the influence of others' opinions, you would probably come up with a much different assessment of whom you are. You would find that you have great qualities that are overlooked, undervalued, or, most often, taken for granted. You will find you are smarter than most people think, kinder than most people know, and have abundant talent in areas that remain hidden from all those around you.

Only you know there is a world-class singer inside of you. A few people at church may know it, but until you do that solo on first Sunday, no one will truly know what kind of pipes you possess. Only you know that you have the great American novel embedded deep within your psyche and no one will ever get a chance to read it until you put pen to paper. You are the only one who knows you can make those around you better people just by talking to them because you never opened your mouth to lend your opinion or advice to their situations.

You have to simply believe in yourself.

There are no two ways about this. When your pastor is in the pulpit speaking to you, he is speaking to you in general. He is speaking to the common elements we all have: the work day, the bills, the relationship, and the family. He doesn't speak to "you" in a way that is personal and unique to you. God created a material that is 10 millimeters wide and six feet long called a double helix. Only three percent of this double helix contains the instructions needed to build your physical body from your hair follicles to your toenails.

From the timbre of your voice to your particular stride that slightly resembles your mother's, this material, called DNA, is uniquely yours. Unless you are a twin or multiple, there are 7 billion others on this planet without your particular sequence of DNA information built into their lives.

I am saying this to point to the fact that you are a unique individual, and God created you uniquely for a reason. If you were supposed to be like everyone else, He never would have made the billions of other unique versions. This tells me, and should tell you, that you should follow the implied instructions to be unique, to act uniquely, and to live a unique life.

So far in life, you have been conditioned to be as much like others as possible and the effect of this is drowning out the uniqueness that is within you. There are other words for unique such as exceptional, outstanding, different, and special. These words inherently describe you because God made you that way all the way down to your DNA. So I implore you to act upon this gift of uniqueness God has given us all. ACT UPON YOUR UNIQUENESS! This will be a challenge because, again, we have been conditioned to not be unique.

Acting on your uniqueness is unique in and of itself. The few of us who act on our God-given uniqueness often find ourselves famous, wealthy, or more importantly, happy. We find that when we follow our uniqueness, we feel absolutely content and happy.

In the example of pop singer Beyonce, her unique combination of light-heartedness, beauty, and her ability to dance, sing, and perform is special, but her added inclination to be in front of a crowd without fear is even more unique as many of us can sing and dance but have a deathly case of stage fright. Because everyone around her supported her uniqueness, she was able to live her life from the beginning believing in herself.

Think of a unique trait within you that you've suppressed for fear of ridicule or lack of support. Then question if you were to tell your family and friends about this unique talent, would you have their support wholeheartedly? What if they gave you encouragement, advice, and they wrote checks too?!

Imagine what your life would be like in that scenario compared to what it is like now. What if you used your unique, God-given self in a way that you thought was best rather than what everyone expected of you? Take a moment and think about that. Does it make you smile inside? If it does, then now is the perfect time for you to reconsider in who and what you believe.

Deion Sanders is considered the greatest football player in his position in the history of the game. In spite of the greatness in his position, he played two other positions on offense and defense. He did as well as, and even better than, the average player in the National Football League (NFL), which consisted of the best of the best football players in the world. Positions he played in the NFL were ones he had never played in high school or college. When he began his NFL career as a first-round draft pick with the Atlanta Falcons, the team offered him $400,000, but he rejected the offer and asked for $11 million.

Sanders had signed with the New York Yankees a year before signing with the Falcons, making him the only player ever to score a touchdown and hit a home run in the same week – the touchdown coming within the first five minutes he had ever played in an NFL game. After an extended NFL and Major League Baseball career, which enriched him to the tune of $100 million, he moved into a career in sports broadcasting as an anchor on a prime time sports series and is considered one of the most dynamic to ever do that job.

Sanders ranks #8 in college football players of all time, #37 in pro football players of the century, and #74 in the greatest athletes of the century. He also played in a World Series and two Super Bowls (the only man to do both). He married a model, has five beautiful kids, produced a platinum-selling album on his record label, recorded several rap singles, wrote an autobiography, and produced a successful reality TV program. He accomplished all this coming from the tiny city of North Fort Myers, Fla.

Although Deion Sanders is not known for his correct use of the English language, his personal philosophy is one of the most powerful there is, and I have adopted it as my own: "If you don't believe in yourself, ain't nobody will!"

What Sanders is saying is true in every sense. If you don't believe in yourself, your uniqueness, and the inner desires you have for your life, you will forever remain beholden to the ideas, assumptions, limitations, and lack of uniqueness others have in their lives. People tend to project their versions of you onto you, and you tend to accept their views as your own. I know this sounds strange, but you and I both know it is absolutely true.

Your friends and relatives should be a source of motivation, inspiration, and encouragement. They should provide you with a space where you can get advice, unload baggage, and seek personal growth. They should not be your source for interpretation of your uniqueness. They cannot interpret your uniqueness as it relates to you and only you. You are the only one who can determine what is best for you as it relates to living your best life possible. No one can truly understand the uniqueness that is shared between God and you alone.

To be fair, wisdom is found in the words of those who have valuable experiences, but there is a code written literally by the hand of God within you that is 100% yours and yours alone. I implore you to act on it now. I implore you to not measure or seek advice in the pursuit of your uniqueness, as no one would understand until you express it fully.

Once you do what God has implied that you do and express your uniqueness and share it with the world, then and only then will the world understand it. Your uniqueness is masked without accompanying action. Once acted upon, somehow they always "knew you had in you."

Imagine your eight-year-old daughter telling you her dreams to become the greatest entertainer since Michael Jackson, but you have it clearly in your mind that she is going to become a doctor, a lawyer, or something. However, when she forms the most successful girl group ever and becomes one of the most successful solo female artists of all time, you "always knew she had it in her."

Beyonce is you. Deion Sanders is you. You know you have it in you. The challenge now is to believe in your uniqueness, believe in what you have inside, and, in time, just as Deion said, others will believe in you as well. This is the ultimate message given to you by God...no pastor required.

If Reginald Lewis' grandfather was told in the 1950s that Little Reggie would orchestrate the largest leveraged buyout in the history of the world, he would've thought they were absolutely crazy. For that matter, if anyone were to be told that Reginald Lewis from Baltimore, MD would go on to Harvard Law School and become America's first Black Billionaire, he or she would consider it foolish. These events hinged upon Reginald's uniqueness. The fact is that when Reginald Lewis bought Beatrice Foods International in a billion dollar buyout and nearly every food commercial on television ended with a woman's voice and tagline reading "We're Beatrice," everyone "knew" he had it in him.

Where NOT to Find a Good Black Man

If you look at any black church in this country, you will find that the overwhelming majority of the congregation is women. Of course, there are some men, often quite a few. But if you look closely you'll find that they are typically old, married, or gay. Just take a look around your church and you will most likely find this to be the case.

You may say to yourself, "That's not true! Brother Smith ain't gay!" However, if you notice, you've never seen him with a woman, he's approaching forty, has no kids, and he wears pink more often than you do. Every gay person isn't flamboyantly so, but we have already covered that.

Taking into consideration that the pastor is often handsome, well-dressed, well-spoken, powerful, and an authority figure, it makes sense that the church is made up of mostly women and single ones, at that. When dealing at the subconscious level, which is always in action, the fact is that the archetype of a husband is a man who has himself together, looks good, speaks well, and gives you direction in your life.

In the absence of a husband, you are describing your pastor. Again, you may refute this claim by saying "not all pastors are men" and this is true, but most of them are.

I'm suggesting pastors are surrogate husbands for single women that flock to the church in droves. He stands in the place of the husband they don't have, and they want the pastor to give them direction, moral support, and, in a lot of cases, serve as eye candy. Sure, the church offers an oasis at the end of a hard work week and a little booster shot on Wednesdays, but at the root of it all, the pastor is the man in their life, even if only at a subconscious level.

This surrogate husband idea is a great trade-off for the pastors. The pastor offers words of affirmation and encouragement and to a shoulder (alter) on which women can cry. From the pastor, women get the masculine energy they crave in every way but sexually. This then leads women to require only sex from other men they encounter.

The pastor's pews stay filled, but the woman is in a constant mode of recycling men who she thinks are only interested in a sexual relationship. In fact, that is their only value when compared to the attributes of the pastor, even if at a subconscious level. Pastors feed into this by asserting themselves as manly figures in an almost intimate way that leaves Black women wanting.

Further, looking for a husband in church is an exercise in futility. For those women seeking a husband in church, I imagine you would do better at the local sports bar because, as I said before, the single men in your church don't want anything from you except chitchat and gossip.

As we all know, single Black men DON'T go to church nearly as much as single Black women and don't go for the same reason that women DO. At church, there is a handsome, well-dressed man standing on stage telling you how to live your life. A heterosexual man neither wants nor requires another man to tell him how to lead his life.

The Church Is a Hunting Ground

While working on a biobehavioral health study (HIV/AIDS) in the late 90s, I conducted surveys and anonymous interviews of young men and women in three large churches in Atlanta, GA. I found what many gay men already know: the church is a hunting ground for single gay men. In fact, this is so common that there are groups of men who frequent the church in much the same way that men frequent night clubs and bars – in search of sex.

This may come as a shock to you, but this is a well-known fact in the gay community. These "hunters" will attend a church for several weeks making acquaintances and having sexual liaisons of some sort only to move on to the next church in search of fresh prey. This behavior is so prominent, in fact, that it is considered by those in the HIV/AIDS education community to be a high-risk behavior even though it can't be presented as such in the literature.

So the idea of finding a good man in church is a myth. Maybe it was true in your grandmother's day, but you can forget that now. Heterosexual, SINGLE men don't go to church in large numbers, and gay men don't want you.

The Man Is the Head of the Household

American culture is Western European culture in which men are the heads of the household. This is true in word and deed - unlike African American households where this is true in word alone. We all know that the man runs the Black household publicly and the woman runs it privately. This is how it has been in African culture and it continues to be so in today's African American culture.

The problem is that the Black man sometimes believes that he really is running the household and forgets that his function is the maintenance of his woman and family. This causes conflict in the household but not nearly as much as Black women behaving as men or "role switching."

Role switching is a survival strategy developed during slavery when the black man could not have contact with the white world in roles of negotiation, business transactions, or any other direct form of communication unless as a proxy of another white man. Black women, on the other hand, acted as proxy or as direct negotiators with white men both at home and in town dealing with merchants.

As previously mentioned in this book, Black women learned to emulate and incorporate the male patterns of communication and behavior to facilitate their daily responsibilities. So, it became common place that white men and Black women were the two dominant race/gender roles in slave society, and these positions continue today.

If you study any corporate environment, you'll find it is led by white men and managed by Black women. White women have been relegated to property and many Black men have been rendered invisible except in the mail room and the cafeteria.

This positioning has led to a dangerous pattern of role switching wherein Black women, while using their deft ability to communicate with white males to succeed at work, damage or even ruin their relationships at home by displaying those same behaviors. They challenge their men by being the head of household and acting as head of household, rendering the Black man invisible once again - this time, in his own home.

This contradicts what Black women's pastors tell them because while he's preaching the man is the head of the household and should be respected as such, all the while the women are displaying completely different behaviors. They know they can't challenge the pastor, so when he talks, they listen.

Meanwhile, back at home, the role switching behavior that is so effective at work prevents the Black woman from allowing her man to act as head of household while she makes real decisions through persuasion and compromise. It causes her to relate to him in the man-to-man scenario in which she's accustomed to participating 40-50 hours a week. In effect, the household becomes one with two men in it, and that's not what a man wants. So, if you behave at home in much the same way you do at work, your man will no longer want to deal with you, and this may eventually lead to the dissolution of the relationship.

This is a subject Black pastors will not touch with a ten-foot pole. If they did address this issue as a problem in the household, their numbers would decrease significantly because women would have a husband at home to call their own.

In some cases, pastors even promote this type of behavior, as I witnessed myself in a prominent Atlanta church headed by a pastor recently embroiled in a homosexual sex scandal. He said he would send a "goon squad" to come and move your husband out of the house if he is unemployed, underemployed, or not "measuring up" to some arbitrary standard of what a husband is. If this implies to the women of his congregation that they need to compare their men to their pastor, then a lot of brothers are going to be moving into studio apartments.

Time out to rest your mind

The world will keep spinning if you take some time off! You must honor yourself long enough to find out who you are and what the hell you want! First and foremost, turn off the tape recorder – the one that keeps you up at night with the endless thoughts of the day and tomorrow.

The Best Kind of Man

The Best Kind of Man

Myths abound about what a 'good Black Man' is, but somehow you can't seem to find one! Truth is, you may be looking for the wrong thing! Instead of looking for what Hollywood and the fashion industry have defined as a good man, you should consider defining him for yourself. By this I mean don't think of the physical and material factors to be the most important things to consider when choosing a man.

The fact is, the physical and material things can be changed and often are. Average-looking men can become good-looking and struggling brothers can become materially successful – both can be accomplished with minor tweaks in lifestyle. Personality, on the other hand, cannot so easily be altered. If the man you are seeing is boring or into things that do not interest you, you are stuck. If lack of communication or humor is a trait he possesses, there is probably not much you can do to change that.

The reality is that no matter what the person looks like or how wealthy they are, you cannot spend time with their looks or their money. You cannot get around the fact that he is mean-spirited or selfish. The bad habits he possesses should not be ignored for the sake of his more than adequate love-making skills.

Time spent with your significant other is much more involved than looking at him or making love to him. There is talking, compromising, laughing, sleeping, eating, partying, family time, child-rearing, nurturing, vacationing, and retiring that must be done together. Imagine doing all that with a man who has the personality of a cardboard box – for the next 50 years! Even worse, imagine doing all these things with a man you cannot bear being around.

Black Men:

The nightmare scenario where two attractive and wealth-oriented people get together and cannot bear to be around each other because of personality conflict is all too common. This can be avoided by choosing your man wisely. Choose your man based on the things that truly matter in life – not the fact that he is a doctor.

You should do an assessment of personality traits that you know are compatible with you and you ways. Do not confuse this with seeking a man with the character traits that "sound good", but the traits that are most compatible with you. For example:

- **His sense of humor – do you guys laugh easily and often?**
- **His personal morals – do you guys agree on right and wrong?**
- **His communication – does he talk freely and easily enough?**

- What matters – does his important things in life sit well with you?
- His goals – does he have a life in mind that is okay with you?

These are the things that actually matter. Not looks that fade or money that becomes not so special once you have plenty of it. What matters is DO YOU LIKE HIM. That is what matters.

Black Men:

Getting Your Man!

Bringing it all together! Getting the love you have been wanting for so long – the easy way!

The Underdeveloped Black Man

By "underdeveloped, I mean the brother that has yet to realize himself as a fully functioning man. The man that was described as a "grown child" earlier in this book is the "underdeveloped" man I speak of. Many women today have relationships with this kind of man and you may be one. Until he can evolve and grow, hopefully with your support, you have to be able to preserve your sanity in the mean time. The key is to alter your perception.

Notice and focus on the good things in every person. Look for ONLY those things. Stop blaming or criticizing anybody you know or run across in life. Keep in mind that you are going to see the best in everything and everyone. Free yourself of the responsibility of trying to make other people the way you wish them to be. Your attention will be on the positive aspects of others and actually brings more value to the people in your life. Do not expect others to behave in a way you want, for the sake of your happiness, as this is both selfish and unrealistic.

Mental Action Plan
a. Understand yourself and Black men
b. Accept the reality of our past as an effect on today's behaviors
c. Tabula Rasa – adopt a blank slate attitude when it comes to meeting men
d. See the real treasure – notice the unique qualities Black men usually possess that can found nowhere else
e. Finish the job of preparing him for you – you won't regret it!

The Numbers Game

Companies have to pay for the postage, paper, computers, mailing lists, and employees' wages to send pieces of direct advertising to your mailbox in hopes that you respond to the ad so they can, in turn, sell some product or service. We label this "junk mail" and tend to treat it as such. In fact, almost 97% of this cost and effort goes straight from the mailbox to the trash can, and the outcome is still considered a success.

I do not prefer this type of advertising and you probably don't either, but the thinking behind it can make for a great example when it comes to relationships, particularly African American relationships. The basic idea is that even with an overwhelming level of failure, the process is still worth undertaking. If you have a man now or have a man later, you still have a man. If you give up, give out, or give in, you run the risk of living alone for the rest of your life.

If you notice, you see this same play on the numbers in all sorts of fields. Taking his into account, it should make sense that the numbers approach must be a valid strategy. Conversely, the intuitive strategy of aiming at a specific desired objective is so often wrong.

Most people hate to fail, and for good reason. Back in the day when we lived out in the open and off the land, failure in battle or in the hunt could mean starving to death, being chastised by our family or tribe, or being fatally injured. This was our reality recently enough that our brains haven't grown and evolved past this fear of failure yet. The instinctual fear of failure is what so often prevents us from taking risks, which, in turn, prevents us from finding success.

But as we all know, failure is a guarantee with most endeavors that are worth trying. To achieve success in the areas in life that we most care about - money, business, happiness and love – the chances of disappointment are so high you may well wonder why anyone bothers. Well, we bother because the satisfaction attained from achieving success far outweighs the disappointment of failure.

This explains why so many people approach achievement in the way they do. They try so hard to avoid loss and disappointment that sure things seem like the only reward worth chasing. They invest all their time, emotions, money, and effort into pursuing the one particular prize they envision as the "best" option for them. When that investment fails, offering little or nothing in return, as the hunt for the top prizes often does, the impact can be devastating.

How many times have you heard sentiments like the following expressed?

"There are no good Black men out there"

"I am fine being alone forever"

"I am not settling I would rather be alone"

Comments like these are what you likely hear from people who've tried love a time or six and failed. Their strategy for success is like someone running a direct mail campaign by sending out only five letters. People like these envision those that achieve their goals as those who've tried and succeeded without much loss. But they've got it all wrong.

"I wasted so much of my life on trying to change men, convince men, and cater to men and here I am alone," is the thought-process.

Success in love, just as in direct mail, is often a numbers game. Even if you have a success rate of one or two percent, it means success! The idea is to make enough attempts to get those one or two percentage points.

When considering the great businessmen that have built large corporations or amassed great fortune, I always think of the many times they failed before making anything that worked. They never gave up because they knew that every success is a numbers game.

Most people I know who have successful long-term relationships have a past filled with as much rejection as all of us have. They tried and struggled their way through the difficult dating scene, and eventually got what was best for them. They played the numbers game and it worked.

Some people will think "Why don't I eliminate all of the 99 % of the failure and just get to the 1% success that would be my husband"? My reply would be to just find out who "he" is and give him a call. If that works for you, give me the winning numbers for the lottery while you are at it!

Direct mail marketers create lists of potential customers that have all the right factors for their products by using predictive modeling. In spite of that preparation they still get only a tiny percentage of the target market. So, even the experts have little idea about what will work and what won't. But they go full steam to reap the rewards of trying to accomplish their desired outcome, knowing full well that the vast majority of their effort will be wasted. Don't be afraid to waste some of your time while working toward that man, it will be worth the wait. Besides, life experiences are never wasted.

Conclusion

Understanding is the key to undoing this pattern of loveless lifestyles our community. Read this book for specific understanding and engage in reflective thought about how some of these topics have affected your love life, your relationship with you father, or your child's father. From there you can begin to reevaluate and redirect your relationships with the men in your life.

It is actually a lot simpler than you think right now. Once you engage in the process of "making it right" and getting the love you deserve, everything will get in the groove of your new direction and flow accordingly. Trust my words, your life is about to change for the better and this change will last forever.

Black Men:

Recommended Viewing

Instead of a reading list, I am recommending a viewing list. This list is comprised of films that, in some way, capture a component of the book and expresses it through the visual art of the big screen. This way is a form of "edu-tainment" or learning while enjoying a good film.

The Color Purple
Baby Boy
Sankofa
The Feast of All Saints
Boys in the Hood
Claudine
South Central
Two Can Play That Game
Why Did I Get Married

Share Your thoughts and Comments

Go To:

www.BlackMenBook.com

Black Men:

References

Akbar, N. (1990). *Chains and images of psychological slavery*. New Jersey: New Mind Productions.

Barras, J. R. (2000). *Whatever happened to daddy's little girl?* New York: Ballantine.

Bartholomew, K. (1990). Avoidance of intimacy: an attachment perspective. *Journal of Social and Personal Relationships, 7*, 147–178.

Bartholomew, K., & Horowitz, L. M. (1991). Attachment styles among young adults: A test of a four-category model. *Journal of Personality and Social Psychology, 61*, 226–244.

Blassingame, J. (1979). *The slave community*. New York: Oxford University Press.

Bogle, D. (1992). *Toms, coons, mulattoes, mammies, and bucks.* New York: Continuum.

Brannon, R. (1976). The male sex role: Our culture's blueprint of manhood, and what it's done for us lately. In D. David & Brannon R. Brannon (Eds.), *The forty-nine percent majority.* Addison Wesley.

Brennan, K. A., Clark, C. L., & Shaver, P. R. (1998). Self-report measurement of adult romantic attachment: An integrative overview. In J. A. Simpson & W. S. Rholes (Eds.), *Attachment theory and close relationships* (pp. 46–76). New York: Guilford Press.

Cazenave, N. A. (1981). Black men in America: The quest for 'manhood. In H. McAdoo (Ed.), *Black families.* Newbury Park, CA: Sage.

Chapman, A. (1995). *Getting good loving.* New York: Ballantine Books.

Clatterbaugh, K. (1990). *Contemporary perspectives on masculinity.* Boulder, CO: Westview Press.

Cross, Jr., W. E. (1998). Black psychological functioning and the legacy of slavery. In Y. Danieli, Ed.) International handbook of multigenerational legacies of trauma (pp. 387-402). New York: Plenum Press.

Danieli, Y. (1998). *International Handbook of Multigenerational Legacies of Trauma.* New York: Plenum Press.

Davis, A. Y. (1983). *Women, race & class.* New York: Vintage Books.

Diop, C. A. (1991). *Civilization or barbarism: An authentic anthropology.* Brooklyn, NY: Lawrence Hill Books.

Diop, C. A. (1978). *The cultural unity of black africa: The domains of patriarchy and matriarchy in classical antiquity.* Chicago: Third World Press.

Dixon, P. (2002). *We want for our sisters what we want for ourselves.* Decatur, GA: Oji Publications.

Doyle, A. J. (1983). *The male experience.* Dubuque, IA: Wm. C. Brown Company.

Dubois, W. E. B. (1909). *The Negro American family.* New York: Schocken Books.

Du Bois, W. E. B. (1986). *The souls of Black folk.* Library of America,

Equiano, O. (1969). The life of Olauduah Equiano or Gustavus Vasa, the African. In A. Bontempts (Ed.), *Great slave narratives* (pp. 1–192). Boston: Beacon Press.

Franklin, D. (1997). *Ensuring inequality.* New York: Oxford University Press.

Frazier, E. F. (1966). *The Negro family in the United States.* Chicago: University of Chicago Press.

Garner, T. (1998). Understanding oral rhetorical practices in African American cultural practices. In V. J. Ducan (Ed.), *Towards achieving MAAT* (pp. 29–44). Dubuque, IA: Kendall-Hunt.

Genovese, E. D. (1972). *Roll, Jordan, roll: The world the slaves made.* New York: Pantheon.

Giddings, P. (1984). *When and where I enter: The impact of Black women on race and sex in America.* New York: Bantam Books.

Glasgow, D. G. (1980). *The Black underclass.* New York: Vintage Books.

Gray, J. (1992). *Men are from Mars, women are from Venus.* New York: Harper-Collins.

Gutman, H. G. (1976). *The Black family in slavery and freedom, 1750–1926.* New York: Vintage Books.

Hacker, A. (1992). *Two Nations: Black and white, separate, hostile, unequal.* New York, NY: Macmillan publishing Company.

Hannerez, U. (1969). *Soulside*. New York: Columbia University Press

Hazan, C., & Shaver, P. R. (1987). Romantic love conceptualized as an attachment process. *Journal of Personality and Social Psychology, 52*, 511–524.

Hill-Collins, P. (2001). *Black feminist thought*. New York: Routledge.

Hill, R. B. (1999). *The strengths of African American families*. Lanham, MD: University Press of America.

Holmes, J. (1993). *John Bowbly and attachment theory*. New York: Routledge.

hooks, b. (1991). *Ain't I a woman: Black women and feminism*. Boston: South End Press.

Johnson, R. (1996). Boys and fatherhood. *In Fathers Families and Communities*. Sacramento, CA.

Jordan, W. D. (1974). *The White man's burden*. Oxford: Oxford University Press.

Ki-Zerbo, G., & Ki-Zerbo, J. (Ed.), *General history of Africa Vol.1: Methodology and African prehistory* (pp. 166–203). California: UNESCO.

Kimmel, M. S. (1995). Introduction. In M. S. Kimmel (Ed.), *The politics of manhood*. Philadelphia, PA: TempleUniversity Press.

Knox, D., & Schacht, C. (2002). *Choices in relationships*. Belmont, CA: Wadsworth.

Leigh, W. (2010). Retirement Savings Behavior and Expectations of African Americans: 1998 and 2009. Washington. Joint Center for Political and Economic Studies.

Leigh, W. (2010). Explaining the Racial/Ethnic Wealth Gap Washington. Joint Center for Political and Economic Studies.

Lerner, G. (1992). *Black women in White America*. New York: Vintage Books.

Love, P., & Robinson, J. (1995). *Hot monogamy*. New York: Plume.

Luquet, W. (1996). *Short-term couples therapy: The imago theory in action.* New York: Brunner/Mazel.

Madhubuti, H. R. (1990). *Black men: Obsolete, single, dangerous.* Chicago: The World Press.

Majors, R., & Billson, J. M. (1992). *Cool pose: The dilemmas of Black manhood in America.* New York: LexingtonBooks.

Mazrui, A. A. (1986). *The African: A Triple Heritage.* Boston: Little, Brown and Company.

McAdoo, H. P. (1997). Upward mobility across generations in African American families. In H. P. McAdoo (Ed.), *Black families* (3rd ed., pp. 139–162). Thousand Oaks, CA: Sage.

Moynihan, D. P. (1965). The Negro family: A case for national action. In W. L. Y. L. Rainwater (Ed.), *The Moynihan report and the politics of controversy* (pp. 41124). Cambridge, MA: The MIT press.

Oliver, M. L., &. Shapiro. T. A. (1997). *Black wealth/White wealth*. New York: Routledge.

Oliver, W. (1989). Sexual conquests and patterns of Black-on-Black violence: A structural-cultural perspective. *Violence and victims, 4*, 257–272.

Pleck, E. H., & Pleck, J. H. (1980). *The American man*. Englewood Cliffs, NJ: Prentice Hall.

N. Hare & J. Hare (Eds.), *Crisis in Black Sexual politics*. Black Think Tank.

Simmons, T., & O'Connell, M. (2003). *Married-couple and unmarried-partner households: 2000*. Washington, D.C.: U.S. Department of Commerce, Economics and Statistics Administration.

Stampp, K. M. (1956). *The peculiar institution: Slavery in the ante-bellum South*. New York: Knopf.

Staples, R. (1999). *The Black family*. New York: Wadsworth.

Sudarkasa, N. (1997). African American families and family values. In H. P. McAdoo (Ed.), *Black families* (3rd ed., pp. 9–40).

Tannen, D. (1990). *You just don't understand*. New York: Ballantine Books.

U.S. Census Bureau. (2005 – 2009). www.census.gov.

U.S. Department of Education (2009). www.census.gov.

Unknown. (1999). *The Willie Lynch letter & the making of a slave*. Chicago: Lushena Books.

White, D. G. (1985). *Ar'n't I a woman?* New York: W. W. Norton.

Williams, C. (1987). *The destruction of the Black civilization*. Third World Press.

Williams, R. (1981). *The collective Black mind: An Afro-centric theory of black personality*. St. Louis, MO: Williamsn & Associates.

Wilson, W. J. (1996). *When work disappears*. New York: Alfred A. Knopf.

Woodson, C. G. (1936). *The African background outlined*.

Washington, D.C.: Association for the Study of Negro Life.

Black Men:

Bibliography

Made in the USA
Charleston, SC
11 July 2012